Revival
Let It Rain

by
Vickie Bryan

Copyright 2019

All rights reserved. No part of this publication may be reproduced without the prior permission of the publisher.

This book is protected by United States copyright laws.

Scripture reference in this book are taken from THE HOLY BIBLE, NEW INTERNATIONAL VERSION®, NIV® Copyright © 1973, 1978, 1984, 2011 by Biblica, Inc.™ Used by permission. All rights reserved worldwide.

Scripture quotations taken from the New American Standard Bible® marked (NASB), Copyright © 1960, 1962, 1963, 1968, 1971, 1972, 1973,

1975, 1977, 1995 by The Lockman Foundation Used by permission. (www.Lockman.org)

Scripture quotations marked "KJV" are taken from the Holy Bible, King James Version, Cambridge, 1769.

Scripture quotations marked (NLT) are taken from the Holy Bible, New Living Translation, copyright © 1996, 2004, 2007 by Tyndale House Foundation. Used by permission of Tyndale House Publishers, Inc., Carol Stream, Illinois 60188. All rights reserved.

Scripture texts in this work are taken from the New American Bible, revised edition © 2010, 1991, 1986, 1970 Confraternity of Christian Doctrine, Washington, D.C. and are used by permission of the copyright owner. All Rights Reserved.

Scriptures marked ISV are taken from the INTERNATIONAL STANDARD VERSION (ISV): Scripture taken from INTERNATIONAL STANDARD VERSION, copyright© 1996-2008 by the ISV Foundation. All rights reserved internationally.

Scriptures marked TM are taken from the THE MESSAGE: THE BIBLE IN

CONTEMPORARY ENGLISH (TM): Scripture taken from THE MESSAGE: THE BIBLE IN CONTEMPORARY ENGLISH, copyright©1993, 1994, 1995, 1996, 2000, 2001, 2002. Used by permission of NavPress Publishing Group

"Scripture quotations taken from the Amplified® Bible, Copyright © 1954, 1958, 1962, 1964, 1965, 1987 by the Lockman Foundation Used by permission.(www.Lockman.org) The Message is quoted: "Scripture taken from The Message. Copyright © 1993, 1994, 1995, 1996, 2000, 2001, 2002. Used by permission of NavPress Publishing Group."

"Scripture quotations are from the ESV® Bible (The Holy Bible, English Standard Version®), copyright © 2001 by Crossway, a publishing ministry of Good News Publishers. Used by permission. All rights reserved."

Scripture quoted by permission. Quotations designated (NET) are from the NET Bible® copyright ©1996-2016 by Biblical Studies Press, L.L.C.http://netbible.org All rights reserved.

V Ly Publishing LLC

1046 Church Rd, W 106-224

Southaven, MS 38671

Print
ISBN: 978-1-942484-01-1

Table of Contents

Introduction 7
Chapter 1 The Call Won't Be Easy 9
Chapter 2 It Doesn't Always Make Sense 11
Chapter 3 Sowing and Reaping 13
Chapter 4 Sow to Yourselves in Righteousness 17
Chapter 5 Reap in Mercy 21
Chapter 6 Break Up Your Fallow Ground 23
Chapter 7 Seek the Lord 27
Chapter 8 We Need the Rain 29
Chapter 9 The Righteous Rain of Revival 33
Chapter 10 Righteousness and Justice 35
Chapter 11 You Are the One 39
Chapter 12 National Revival 45
Chapter 13 The Cycle of Work and Rest 49
Chapter 14 Restoration in His Presence 53
Chapter 15 Waking Up Dormant Ground 57
Chapter 16 An Appointed Time 61
Chapter 17 A Promise to Revive 65
Chapter 18 Restoration 67
Chapter 19 The Former and Latter Rain 69
Chapter 20 Let It Rain 75

Introduction

Is time ticking away with your God given dreams left unfulfilled? Have you given up? Well, I can identify with this. One evening the Lord spoke to my heart: "Break up your fallow ground." So I grabbed my Bible to find out exactly what he wanted to reveal. In Hosea 10:12, I found the scripture:

> *Sow to yourselves in righteousness, reap in mercy; break up your fallow ground: for [it is] time to seek the LORD, till he come and rain righteousness upon you. Hosea 10:12 KJV*

Inspiration for scripture originates from God, and Hosea 10:12 contains the keys of what I believe brings revival. While God works for our good, the enemy works against us. At times we turn from faith to frustration and discouragement. People backslide, sit down, and quit. In such circumstances a revival becomes necessary. Revival is "an instance of returning to life or consciousness; restoration of vigor, vitality; or a renewed use."1

Antonyms for revival such as "depress, discourage and dishearten reveal where many find themselves." 2 When these symptoms show up, the reader needs revival.

> *For thus says the high and exalted One Who lives forever, whose name is Holy, "I dwell on a high and holy place, And also with the contrite and lowly of spirit In order to revive the spirit of the lowly and to revive the heart of the contrite. Isaiah 57:15 (NASB)*

When the Lord spoke to me, "Break up your fallow ground," I was not backslidden, but I remained so unfulfilled in my life's destiny (Hosea 10:12). One could say I had a crushed spirit. Something needed to change and it was me. The Lord knew what I needed, I needed a revival. Not only will revival change one's life, it will change a nation. To all who read and take hold of the truth in this book, hang on because revival is on the way.

1. Dictionary.com Unabridged. Random House, Inc. 20 Mar. 2016. <Dictionary.comhttp://www.dictionary.com/browse/revive>.

2. " revive ". Roget's 21st Century Thesaurus, Third Edition. Philip Lief Group 2009. 01 Sep. 2016. <Thesaurus.comhttp://www.thesaurus.com/browse/ revive >.

3. The LORD is close to the brokenhearted and saves those who are crushed in spirit. Psalm 34:18

Revival Let It Rain

Chapter 1

The Call Won't Be Easy

Fulfillment of ones divine destiny comes out of a relationship with the Lord. One must hear from God and walk in obedience to his word. This does not guarantee it will work out the way we desire. Hosea's ministry came at a difficult time in Israel. People who supposedly knew the Lord no longer acted like it. So the Lord sought a man to be his change agent. He sent his word to Hosea.

> *1 The word of the Lord that came to Hosea son of Beeri during the reigns of Uzziah, Jotham, Ahaz and Hezekiah, kings of Judah, and during the reign of Jeroboam son of Jehoash king of Israel. Hosea 1:1*

As soon as Hosea stepped into the office of a prophet, God set the stage for his ministry. The prophet's life would be a sign to Israel. Once a faithful nation to the Lord, Israel had changed. Israel's relationship turned adulterous, just as unfaithfulness in a marriage. Israel became like the other nations who never knew God. Then the word of the Lord came to Hosea which began his ministry.

> *When the Lord began to speak through Hosea, the Lord said to him, "Go, marry a promiscuous woman and have children with her, for like an adulterous wife this land is guilty of unfaithfulness to the Lord." Hosea 1:2*

What a peculiar command given to Hosea, but it seems without hesitation he did what God told him. Hosea entered into a marriage covenant with a woman known to be sexually immoral. Hosea could now identify with God's heart to a spiritually immoral nation. With such a marriage, Hosea became a prophet with firsthand understanding of living with an adulterous wife.

Even each child Gomer conceived was given a name of prophetic significance by the Lord (Hosea 1:4-8). The New Living Translation expresses this scripture in a way that explains the condition of God's people.

> *3So he married Gomer daughter of Diblaim, and she conceived and bore him a son. 4Then the Lord said to Hosea, "Call him Jezreel, because I will soon punish the house of Jehu for the massacre at Jezreel, and I will put an end to the kingdom of Israel. 5In that day I will break Israel's bow in the Valley of Jezreel." 6Gomer conceived again and gave birth to a daughter. Then the Lord said to Hosea, "Call her Lo-Ruhamah (which means "not loved"), for I will no longer show love to Israel that I should at all forgive them. 7Yet I will show love to Judah; and I will save them—not by bow, sword or battle, or by horses and horsemen, but I, the Lord their God, will save them." 8After she had weaned Lo-Ruhamah, Gomer had another son. 9Then the Lord said, "Call him Lo-Ammi (which means "not my people"), for you are not my people, and I am not your God. Hosea 1:3-9 NLT*

Gomer conceived three children while married to Hosea. The first son, Jezreel, was Hosea's biological child (Hosea 1:3). The second child could have been as well. Scripture does not identify her specifically as Hosea's. The third child's conception most likely occurred through prostitution. "Gomer had another son" (Hosea 1:8). With unfaithfulness present in this relationship, the question of paternity arises. So we do not know for sure.

Over time the Lord continued to speak through Hosea as he addressed Israel. As most prophets, Hosea did not back down on speaking the truth given him by the Lord.

Vickie Bryan

Chapter 2

It Doesn't Always Make Sense

In Hosea chapter 3, the Lord spoke to the prophet to go to his adulterous wife once again. Gomer no longer lived with Hosea but with another lover. It would even cost him financially to get her back. Hosea the prophet's life was on display.

Imagine Hosea's thoughts as he went to look for Gomer. "The Lord told me to go find my wife, but oh, what I endured with that woman. She's the mother of my children, well maybe." As memories of their life together filled his mind, other thoughts long tucked away emerged. "She loved other men more than she did me. I remember the smell of her perfume and the way she dressed, but it wasn't for me. Everything about Gomer reeked adultery, and I've endured enough with that cheating woman. All that does not matter now, I will obey the Lord." Take note, all this difficulty came as the result of the call on Hosea's life.

Not only was Hosea to redeem her but commanded to love her again. This is God's heart for his children even when they turn from him. I like the Message Bible for this scripture. It reads like people speak today. "Then God ordered me, "Start all over: Love your wife again, your wife who's in bed with her latest boyfriend, your cheating wife. Love her the way I, God, love the Israelite people, even as they flirt and party with every god that takes their fancy." 2-3 I did it. I paid good money to get her back. It cost me the price of a slave. Then I told her, "From now on you're living with me. No more whoring, no more sleeping around. You're living with me and I'm living with you" (Hosea 3:1-3 The Message (MSG)).

Even the amount Hosea paid to redeem his wife was of prophetic significance. A reference from Barnes Notes on the Bible states,

> *'the fifteen shekels were half the price of a common slave' (Exodus 21:32) and so may denote her worthlessness. The homer and half-homer of barley, or forty-five bushels, are nearly the allowance of food for a slave among the Romans, four bushels a month. Barley was the offering of one accused of adultery, and, being the food of animals, betokens that she was 'like horse and mule which have no understanding.'* "[1]

The adulteress wife debased herself with different lovers as the twin nations did with other gods. When unfaithfulness occurs in any relationship, the one betrayed does not easily trust again. I do not think Hosea escaped this human response. As Hosea obeyed God, he made the rules clear to Gomer. Nevertheless, neither Israel nor Judah responded in the manner God longed for.

God desired the love of his people, and, as any good father, he wanted to bless them. Neither Israel nor Judah listened to warnings given by the prophets. They did not turn from sin, so instead of restoration, judgment from heaven did not cease. Hard circumstances gave warning as they continued to ignore God's plea. The further away they moved from God, the worse it got for them. Consequences took away more and more of the blessings of God including liberty and freedom.

If a child continues to go in destructive paths while ignoring parental warnings, what can that parent do? They only thing left would be consequences of actions for that child. This cycle repeated with God and his people. The further they went from the Lord, the worse it got for them. What could God do?

---

[1] "Barnes' Notes on the Bible."

Bible Hub. N.p., n.d. Web. 31 Mar. 2016. <http://biblehub.com/commentaries/hosea/3-2.htm>.

Chapter 3

Sowing and Reaping

All parts of creation move in cycles. A cycle is "any complete round or series of occurrences that repeats or is repeated."1 Just as the cycles of seed time and harvest, day and night, and summer and winter continues, so each cycle ushers in the next. These help maintain the balance God set for life on earth. All life, including mankind, functions within the framework of God's creation. This declares the glory of God as he alone created and put them in place. Sowing and reaping makes up a cycle that also affects our life's destinies.

Judgment from heaven came against Israel and Judah. In Hosea chapter 10, once again God revealed his love and a path for restoration (Hosea 10:12). This in itself constitutes a cycle.

> Sow to yourselves in righteousness, reap in mercy; break up your fallow ground: for it is time to seek the LORD, till he come and rain righteousness upon you. Hosea 10:12 KJV

In Hosea 10:12 the prophet mentions the cycle of sowing and reaping at work upon the earth. The first mention of sowing and reaping, or seed time and harvest, takes us back to the book of Genesis.

> As long as the earth endures, seed time and harvest, cold and heat, summer and winter, day and night will never cease. Genesis 8:22

As revealed in 1 Thessalonians 5:23 each one of us consists of a spirit, soul, and a body.2 As a spirit who lives in a human body, whatever one does will produce seeds. The spirit, soul, and body are a package as each one relates to the other. We cannot ignore our creation and why God made man in the first place. Adam in the garden exemplifies this as God and man were united in spirit. Before his fall, Adam's spirit, soul, and body flowed together. After Adam sinned, his spirit died, and he became a soulish, flesh man ruled by the dictates of both.

What we do will affect us not only physically but spiritually as well. Likewise in a walk with God we go through cycles. Adam sowed the seed of rebellion when he violated the command from God (Genesis 3). Adam's harvest, his spirit, was severed from the spirit of God, and he entered into spiritual death. His body changed from immortal to mortal, which brought physical death. Adam's surroundings changed as well. He was kicked out of the Garden of Eden. The plush garden was replaced with the sweat and toil of working the ground.

Apostle Paul explained it to the New Testament church in Galatians 6:7-8. God cannot be mocked. Plain and simple, a man, woman, or child reaps whatever he or she sows. Seeds are sown not only by our actions but also by the words we speak. As the Bible revealed in Genesis chapter 1, God spoke and creation came into existence. Man, made in God's likeness, must take heed of what we speak. Just like actions, spoken words will create for us either good or bad. (Psalm 33:6, 9)

Various scriptures affirm just how words affect our lives. In Proverbs 18:21, whatever we speak has the power to bring death or life. As the Amplified Bible translates, all of us will "eat the fruit" of our words and "bear the consequences" of them (Proverbs 18:21).

What we say with our tongues can curse or bless ourselves or others. The apostle James understood the power of life and death released by what one says. A tongue without restraint is just as destructive and hard to maintain as a fire (James 3:6). Once the damaging ability of the human tongue is understood, wisdom must be applied. Many wonder why their destinies are stalled and not fulfilled. The laws of God still apply today.

1. "cycle". Dictionary.com Unabridged. Random House, Inc. 28 Sep. 2016. <Dictionary.comhttp://www.dictionary.com/browse/cycle>.
2. May your whole spirit, soul and body be kept blameless at the coming of our Lord Jesus Christ. 1 Thessalonians 5:23

Vickie Bryan

The Keys of Revival

Hosea 10:12

Revival Let It Rain

Chapter 4

Sow to Yourselves in Righteousness

Sow to yourselves in righteousness, reap in mercy; break up your fallow ground: for [it is] time to seek the LORD, till he come and rain righteousness upon you. Hosea 10:12 KJV

Hosea told those who would listen to sow seeds of righteousness. In Hosea 10:12 the word righteousness appears two times. The first, tsĕdaqah, means, "righteousness and justice."1 Tsĕdaqah comes from the Hebrew root word tsadaq, to "plant seeds of righteous (in conduct and character)".2

In Hosea 10:12 tsĕdaqah also denotes rectitude. By definition rectitude means, "rightness of principal or conduct; moral virtue: correctness."3 Synonyms for rectitude highlight what righteousness looks like: "decency, honesty, integrity, morality, probity, goodness and virtue."4 Righteousness is not "corruption, deceit, dishonesty, immorality, evil, infamy" as antonyms for rectitude affirm.5 The second righteousness in Hosea 10:12 (tsedeq) means to "make right, to cleanse, justify." 6

Both Hebrew words for righteousness are from the same root word tsadaq. Righteousness sown will be righteousness reaped as Gods sends his rain into one's life.

I am not talking about righteousness one tries to gain by mere good works. This does not work with a heart far from God. Isaiah explained the value of such works alone without faith in God. "All of us have become like one who is unclean, and all our righteous acts are like filthy rags; we all shrivel up like a leaf, and like the wind our sins sweep us away" (Isaiah 64:6).

Hosea specifically told Israel to stop their evil ways. The process would begin when each person examined themselves and turned to righteousness.

God's children needed to truly turn their hearts back to their righteous God and plant seeds of doing what was right (in conduct and character) according to God's standards. This would be a turning point for any who did so. Why? Due to the reciprocal effects of the law of sowing and reaping. Righteous seeds yield a harvest of God's mercy. Without his mercy, we are without hope.

Think about it. Planting seeds puts them in the ground to produce a harvest. We know a seed will produce according to its kind, and a harvest yields specifically according to the type of seed planted. In Hosea 10:12 we are told to sow "seeds of righteousness." How does one sow righteous seeds? Apostle Paul told the churches in Galatia to "do good" which came with a promise (Galatians 6:9). The promise will come as a blessing to one's life. So what is good (kalos)? In the Greek dictionary kalos means "good, excellent in its nature and characteristics, and therefore well adapted to its ends."7 A dictionary defines good as "morally excellent or admirable; virtuous; righteous." 8 Righteous seeds are good seeds.

As the apostle Paul taught the churches in Galatia, we are not to sow seeds to our sin (flesh) nature but to please the Holy Spirit. (Galatians 6:8) Flesh in this scripture, sarx, "denotes the earthly nature of man apart from divine influence, and therefore prone to sin and opposed to God."9 Paul then explained this type of behavior in Galatians 5:16-21.

> *16So I say, walk by the Spirit, and you will not gratify the desires of the flesh. 17For the flesh desires what is contrary to the Spirit, and the Spirit what is contrary to the flesh. They are in conflict with each other, so that you are not to do whatever you want. 18But if you are led by the Spirit, you are not under the law. 19The acts of the flesh are obvious: sexual immorality, impurity and debauchery; 20idolatry and witchcraft; hatred, discord, jealousy, fits of rage, selfish ambition, dissensions, factions 21 and envy; drunkenness, orgies, and the like. I warn you, as I did before, that those who live like this will not inherit the kingdom of God. Galatians 5:16-21*

These acts of the flesh were just the things Israel and Judah did. Due to such behavior, the individuals as well the nations needed to turn to righteousness. According to the law of sowing and reaping, harvest time will come for all.

> Revival Key #1 - Hosea told God's children to truly turn their hearts back to their righteous God and plant seeds of doing what was right (in conduct and character). The process begins when each person examines themselves and their relationship with the Lord. How is it? Can it be better? Is the reader's relationship with him cold, lukewarm or hot (Rev 3:18)?

1. "H6666 - tsĕdaqah - Strong's Hebrew Lexicon (KJV)." Blue Letter Bible. Web. 28 Mar, 2018. <https://www.blueletterbible.org//lang/lexicon/lexicon.cfm?Strongs=H6666&t=KJV>.

2. "H6663 - tsadaq - Strong's Hebrew Lexicon (KJV)." Blue Letter Bible. Web. 12 Apr, 2016. <https://www.blueletterbible.org//lang/lexicon/lexicon.cfm?Strongs=H6663&t=KJV>.

3. "rectitude". *Dictionary.com Unabridged.* Random House, Inc. 28 Marx 2018.

    <Dictionary.com http://www.dictionary.com/browse/rectitude>.

4. "honor". Roget's 21st Century Thesaurus, Third Edition. Philip Lief Group 2009. 28 Mar. 2018.

    <Thesaurus.com http://www.thesaurus.com/browse/honor>.

5. "rectitude". Roget's 21st Century Thesaurus, Third Edition. Philip Lief Group 2009. 28 Mar. 2018.

    <Thesaurus.com http://www.thesaurus.com/browse/ rectitude >.

6. "H6664 - tsedeq - Strong's Hebrew Lexicon (KJV)." Blue Letter Bible. Web. 28 Mar, 2018. <https://www.blueletterbible.org//lang/lexicon/lexicon.cfm?Strongs=H6664&t=KJV>.

7. "G2570 - kalos - Strong's Greek Lexicon (KJV)." Blue Letter Bible. Web. 28 Mar, 2018. <https://www.blueletterbible.org//lang/lexicon/lexicon.cfm?Strongs=G2570&t=KJV>.

8. "good". Dictionary.com Unabridged. Random House, Inc. 28 Mar. 2018.

    <Dictionary.com http://www.dictionary.com/browse/good>.

9. "G4561 - sarx - Strong's Greek Lexicon (KJV)." Blue Letter Bible. Web. 15 Apr, 2016. <https://www.blueletterbible.org//lang/lexicon/lexicon.cfm?Strongs=G4561&t=KJV>.

Revival Let It Rain

Chapter 5

Reap in Mercy

Sow to yourselves in righteousness, reap in mercy ... Hosea 10:12

After one chooses to sow righteousness, the harvest of mercy follows. Any driver could appreciate this illustration of mercy when a police officer does not issue a deserved ticket. That happened to a fellow believer as a hurried, pushy driver drove too close to his bumper. Uncomfortable with the situation, my friend began to speed. The result was a police officer pulled him over while the pushy driver went by. That seemed so unfair but, thanks to the mercy of God, it did not end that way. As this believer made his way to the side of the road, the Lord spoke, "Ask me to deliver you." The Lord did just that, and the officer gave him a warning and not a ticket. That was the mercy of God. My friend deserved a ticket, but God's "kindness, compassion and favor" came to his rescue.1 The Lord taught him not to allow the impatience of another driver to incite him to speed. We can depend on the Lord who desires to show his mercy.

The best example of mercy occurred when Jesus paid for the sins of all mankind. We sinned, he did not, yet he bore our penalty. We didn't deserve it, but God's mercy displayed itself through "kindness, compassion and favor."2 Not all people turn to righteousness and so, accordingly, do not reap available mercy.

Bible accounts of the rescues of Noah and Lot reveal again just how much we need God's mercy. God destroyed the ancient world but spared Noah and his family. Sodom and Gomorrah also came under God's judgment. The Lord sent his angels to deliver one man and his family, just as he had done for Noah. Both examples display God's mercy toward the righteous. Those who did not choose righteousness were lost. (2 Peter 2:5-9 NLT) Even when

Lot feared he could not run fast enough to escape, his request for a shorter distance was granted. Not only did this request spare Lot's life but a small town as well. (Genesis 19:18-21)

So we see righteousness brings the mercy of God on our behalf. We can depend on God's mercy daily.

22It is of the LORD'S mercies that we are not consumed, because his compassions fail not. 23They are new every morning: great is thy faithfulness.

Another contemporary of Hosea, the prophet Micah, dealt with the tribes of Judah and Benjamin. Micah sounded much like Hosea as he pointed God's people back to him. "He has shown you, O mortal, what is good. And what does the Lord require of you? To act justly and to love mercy and to walk humbly with your God (Micah 6:8). So when an individual turns to righteousness, God turns toward them with a harvest of his mercy. Micah told his audience to "act right" (justly), this is righteousness.3

> Revival Key # 2 - Sow righteousness and the harvest of mercy will surely come one's way.

1. "H6663 - tsadaq - Strong's Hebrew Lexicon (KJV)." Blue Letter Bible. Web. 23 Jun, 2016. <https://www.blueletterbible.org//lang/lexicon/lexicon.cfm?Strongs=H6663&t=KJV>.

2. Ibid

3. "H4941 - mishpat - Strong's Hebrew Lexicon (KJV)." Blue Letter Bible. Web. 5 Sep, 2016. <https://www.blueletterbible.org//lang/lexicon/lexicon.cfm?Strongs=H4941&t=KJV>.

4. The LORD said to me, "You have seen correctly, for I am watching to see that my word is fulfilled." Jeremiah 1:12

Chapter 6

Break Up Your Fallow Ground

Sow to yourselves in righteousness, reap in mercy; break up your fallow ground . . . Hosea 10:12

"Break up your fallow ground" is a command that requires action. So what makes ground fallow? From the dictionary, fallow speaks "(of land) plowed and left unseeded for a season or more; uncultivated."1 The purpose of fallow land lays dormant for a course of time. Does the reader hold onto a vision from long ago that seem to go nowhere? Maybe that particular vision rests on fallow ground?

Hosea was not the only one who prophesied such to God's people. Jeremiah the prophet spoke the same words.

3 For thus saith the LORD to the men of Judah and Jerusalem, Break up your fallow ground, and sow not among thorns. Jeremiah 4:3 KJV

Jeremiah added another important aspect to this command. "Break up your fallow ground, and sow not among thorns" (Jeremiah 4:3). I bet the reader has come across a thorn or two in one's life. Years ago my husband and I planted some seedling trees given to us. Among those trees a thorn bush emerged. If there's anything I highly suggest, be careful around thorns. Trying to mow or pull weeds near it was horrible. Those thorns were treacherous. If I got too close, it hurt. Can the reader imagine putting your hands through a thorn bush to harvest a crop? I don't believe anyone would knowingly plant tomatoes, beans, or anything else among thorns. Thorns, weeds, and the like must go so good seeds can yield a harvest.

Actually, thorns are weeds as well. A weed is defined as a," valueless plant growing wild especially one that grows on cultivated ground to the exclusion or injury of the desired crop".2 In thinking about it, just what does it take to grow weeds? Not much. Has anyone ever had difficulty growing any? Moments ago, I looked down and saw weeds in our flower bed. Weeds grow hardily; after all they are plants too. The difference is weeds are not wanted. As the weeds grow, they suck nutrition from the soil, crowding out desirable plants.3

In the *Parable of the Sower* Jesus also warned of planting seeds among thorns. Thorns obstruct the good things we desire to manifest in our lives.4 In this parable "the seed that fell among thorns stands for those who hear, but as they go on their way they are choked by life's worries, riches and pleasures, and they do not mature" (Luke 8:14). Thorns in scripture may also represent wicked men. "But evil men are all to be cast aside like thorns, which are not gathered with the hand (2 Samuel 23:6). A person who represents a thorn may be a source of one's worries. Not only weeds, but the presence of rocks also poses a problem.

A Rock in a Pot

The crisp fall air encouraged me to bring my houseplants inside. The next day temperatures would rise, but for now inside they went. In a tray of small plants I noticed one much smaller than the others. The dirt looked the same, but upon inspection I felt something hard. It was a rock. Its presence gave my plant nowhere to grow. So this little plant was half the size as the others. It could not grow normally due to the presence of a blockage. Its growth remained limited at best. The same happens to us: rocks hinder and even stop our growth. Rocks as well as thorns must be removed for the desired righteous seed to grow. This is part of breaking up one's fallow ground. To break up one's fallow ground means you must make some changes.

From Easton's Bible Dictionary. Here we find what one must do to "break up your fallow ground" (Hosea 10:12).

> *The expression, "Break up your fallow ground" (Hosea 10:12; Jeremiah 4:3) means, "Do not sow your seed among thorns", i.e., break off all your evil habits; clear your hearts of weeds, in order that they may be prepared for the seed of righteousness. Land was allowed to lie fallow that it might become more fruitful; but when in this condition, it soon became overgrown with thorns and weeds. The cultivator of the soil was careful to "break up" his fallow ground, i.e., to clear the field of weeds, before sowing seed in it. So says the prophet, "Break off your evil ways, repent*

of your sins, cease to do evil, and then the good seed of the word will have room to grow and bear fruit." 5

"Break off your evil ways, repent of your sins, and cease to do evil" are steps of actions to "break up" one's fallow ground.6 Yet people tend to have blind spots concerning themselves.

In this case and always, it takes the ministry of the Holy Spirits to reveal what we do not recognize. If one is sincere in turning to righteousness and breaking up ones fallow ground, then the Holy Spirit's will expose what is hidden. Before Jesus went to the cross, he promised to send us a Helper. In this promise, Jesus described the ministry of the Holy Spirit in John 16:7.

Weeds contain a root system that cannot be seen on the surface. We need the help of the Holy Spirit to expose what's hidden and needs to be removed from the ground of our hearts. Help us, Holy Spirit.

Revival Key #3 - Explore life's worries, riches, and pleasure choking one's fruitfulness." Also with the help of the Holy Spirit examine one's life to reveal any person who may represent a thorn. Make the necessary changes as the Holy Spirits leads.

Revival Key #4 – Forgive - Forgiving others and even ourselves of wrongdoing will set us free. "For if you forgive other people when they sin against you, your heavenly Father will also forgive you. But if you do not forgive others their sins, your Father will not forgive your sins" (Matthew 6:14-15).

1. "fallow". Dictionary.com Unabridged. Random House, Inc. 18 Jul. 2016. <Dictionary.comhttp://www.dictionary.com/browse/fallow>.
2. "2. weed". Dictionary.com Unabridged. Random House, Inc. 26 Jul. 2016. <Dictionary.comhttp://www.dictionary.com/browse/weed>.
3. Ibid.
4. The Parable of the Sower -- 4While a large crowd was gathering and people were coming to Jesus from town after town, he told this parable: 5"A farmer went out to sow his seed. As he was scattering the seed, some fell along the path; it was trampled on, and the birds ate it up. 6Some fell on rocky ground, and when it came up, the plants withered because they had no moisture. 7Other seed fell

among thorns, which grew up with it and choked the plants. 8Still other seed fell on good soil. It came up and yielded a crop, a hundred times more than was sown." 11"This is the meaning of the parable: The seed is the word of God. 12Those along the path are the ones who hear, and then the devil comes and takes away the word from their hearts, so that they may not believe and be saved. 13Those on the rocky ground are the ones who receive the word with joy when they hear it, but they have no root. They believe for a while, but in the time of testing they fall away. 14The seed that fell among thorns stands for those who hear, but as they go on their way they are choked by life's worries, riches and pleasures, and they do not mature. 15But the seed on good soil stands for those with a noble and good heart, who hear the word, retain it, and by persevering produce a crop. Luke 8:4-8;8:11-15

5. Easton, Matthew. "Fallow-Ground - Easton's Bible Dictionary." Blue Letter Bible. 24 Jun, 1996. Web. 15 Jul, 2016. <https://www.blueletterbible.org//search/Dictionary/viewTopic.cfm>.

6. Ibid

Chapter 7

Seek the Lord

[it is] time to seek the LORD... Hosea 10:12c KJV

The next requirements of Hosea's prophesy involves seeking the Lord. This book in the hands of the reader provides such an opportunity. In a dictionary seek is "to try to find or discover by searching or questioning."1 Whenever a need arises, I will do what it takes to fulfill it. If hungry, I will seek food to eat. The hungrier I become the more determined I am to feed my growling stomach. In the same way it takes food to satisfy physical hunger, it takes God to satisfy the spiritual longing in man. There is only one true God, and he alone satisfies us.

To seek dawrash' in Hosea 10:12 specifically means "to seek God by prayer and worship." 2 As the water on the earth evaporates up into the clouds and moves over the earth, our worship and prayers are received by God. In seeking God we find out what hindrances must go. In so doing one's fallow ground can be prepared for God's use. (Deuteronomy 4:29 (ASV))

Nevertheless, some people remain in darkness and do not come to the light because they like sin. If this is the case, God will be ignored. When people get tired of the pain and hardship sin causes, they begin to seek a way out. Many at that time will turn or return to the Lord. (Hosea 5:15 NLT)

Jesus taught his disciples to seek the Kingdom of God and his righteousness. This is the same as Hosea admonished to be done.

> *33 But seek ye first the kingdom of God, and his righteousness; and all these things shall be added unto you. Matthew 6:33 KJV*

Seek in Matthew 6:33 is to "seek in order to find; to crave."[3] Sometimes I get a craving for dark chocolate. My taste buds relish in the thoughts of chocolate melting in my mouth. Similarly, my spirit craves to know the Lord even more. As in Hosea 10:12, God makes it plain what one must do to be restored to him. What one does may come down to how hungry one may be to know him. The benefits are not only eternal but for here and now. I admit when something is important to me, I will go after it with all my heart. My relationship with the Lord is just that. It is the pearl of great price. He is my love and well worth the pursuit.

> Revival Key #5 – Earnestly seek God through prayer and worship.

1. "seek". Dictionary.com Unabridged. Random House, Inc. 24 Jul. 2016. <Dictionary.comhttp://www.dictionary.com/browse/seek>.

2. "H1875 - darash - Strong's Hebrew Lexicon (KJV)." Blue Letter Bible. Web. 24 Jul, 2016. <https://www.blueletterbible.org//lang/lexicon/lexicon.cfm?Strongs=H1875&t=KJV>.

3. "G2212 - zēteō - Strong's Greek Lexicon (KJV)." Blue Letter Bible. Web. 16 Sep, 2016. <https://www.blueletterbible.org//lang/lexicon/lexicon.cfm?Strongs=G2212&t=KJV>.

Vickie Bryan

Chapter 8

We Need the Rain

[It is] time to seek the LORD, till he come and rain righteousness upon you. Hosea 10:12 KJV

As of Genesis 2:5, not one shrub or plant grew upon the earth. Both rain and man were missing at this point. Earth's surface received water, but it did not pour from above. God would send the rain as a prerequisite for what he was about to do.

> *4This is the account of the heavens and the earth when they were created, when the Lord God made the earth and the heavens. 5Now no shrub had yet appeared on the earth and no plant had yet sprung up, for the Lord God had not sent rain on the earth and there was no one to work the ground, 6but streams came up from the earth and watered the whole surface of the ground. 7Then the Lord God formed a man from the dust of the ground and breathed into his nostrils the breath of life, and the man became a living being. 8Now the Lord God had planted a garden in the east, in Eden; and there he put the man he had formed. 9The Lord God made all kinds of trees grow out of the ground—trees that were pleasing to the eye and good for food. 15The Lord God took the man and put him in the Garden of Eden to work it and take care of it. Genesis 2:4-9; 15*

God himself made all the preparations ahead of man's arrival. He planted the garden and caused all kinds of trees "pleasing to the eye and good for food" to grow (Genesis 2:4-9). This set seed time and harvest in motion. By Genesis 2:15 rain obviously fell. We know this since God placed Adam in the garden for the work prepared for him. God sends rain, but man must do his part to yield a harvest. By design the Lord knew shrubs and plants would spring forth after he sent rain. He knows ahead of time what will come, so he looks for a person to fulfill his plan. In the time of Abraham, God needed a man who would hear him and believe. After one responds, then God reveals what is required. Abraham became the father of faith because he did just that: he believed he heard from God. Then he did what the Lord required of him. (Genesis 12:1-4)

Rain in Genesis 2:5 from the Strong's Concordance is the Hebrew word matar which simply means "to rain or to rain upon." 1 Rain yarah in Hosea 10:12 is a different Hebrew word that brings a different understanding to our study. What proves interesting is yarah was translated "to teach" 42 times out of 84 occurrences in scripture. 2 Yarah means "to point out (as if by aiming the finger), to teach: direct, inform, instruct"3 Yarah, "to shoot," appeared 18 times, as to shoot an arrow."4 Bible verses for the Hebrew word yarah will help us recognize this rain which falls from heaven.

Teach

(Yarah)

Teach me your way, Lord, that I may rely on your faithfulness; give me an undivided heart, that I may fear your name. Psalms 86:11

Teach me, LORD, the way of your decrees, that I may follow it to the end. Psalms 119:33

Teach me, and I will hold my tongue: and cause me to understand wherein I have erred. Job 6:24 KJV

I have not departed from your laws, for you yourself have taught me. Psalms 119:102

I instruct you in the way of wisdom and lead you along straight paths. Proverbs 4:11

Shoot

(Yarah)

Usually an archer shoots an arrow with a target in mind. God just as well can shoot rain (yarah) to a targeted recipient.

> *I will shoot three arrows to the side of it, as though I were shooting at a target. 1 Samuel 20:20*

> *…and he said to the boy, "Run and find the arrows I shoot." As the boy ran, he shot an arrow beyond him. 1 Samuel 20:36*

> *For, lo, the wicked bend their bow, they make ready their arrow upon the string that they may privily shoot at the upright in heart. Psalms 11:2 KJV*

> *"But God shall shoot at them with an arrow; suddenly shall they be wounded. Psalms 64:7 KJV*

1. "H4305 - matar - Strong's Hebrew Lexicon (KJV)." Blue Letter Bible. Web. 5 Aug, 2016. <https://www.blueletterbible.org//lang/lexicon/lexicon.cfm?Strongs=H4305&t=KJV>.

2. "H3384 - yarah - Strong's Hebrew Lexicon (KJV)." Blue Letter Bible. Web. 5 Aug, 2016. <https://www.blueletterbible.org//lang/lexicon/lexicon.cfm?Strongs=H3384&t=KJV>.

3. Ibid.Ibid.

Revival Let It Rain

Chapter 9

The Righteous Rain of Revival

> *He causes his sun to rise on the evil and the good, and sends rain on the righteous and the unrighteous. Matthew 5:44*

God sends rain which provides benefit to all. Nevertheless, there exists a type of rain that falls upon the righteous that evades the ungodly.

> *12What we have received is not the spirit of the world, but the Spirit who is from God, so that we may understand what God has freely given us. 13This is what we speak, not in words taught us by human wisdom but in words taught by the Spirit, explaining spiritual realities with Spirit-taught words. 14The person without the Spirit does not accept the things that come from the Spirit of God but considers them foolishness, and cannot understand them because they are discerned only through the Spirit. 1 Corinthians 2:12-14*

In Hosea 10:12 Hosea spoke about what I call a righteous rain. Yarah is this righteous rain. God sends yarah (rain) upon the godly. The ungodly will not benefit from this rain, since they do not receive it. First of all, to benefit from yarah one must believe that he is God. As Hosea 10:12 and Hebrews 11:6 agree, when one earnestly seeks the Lord then the reward comes. Reward in Hebrews 11:6 means, "One who pays wages, a rewarder."1 When one seeks the Lord, he sends yarah rain. Just as wages are paid, the Lord rewards those who earnestly seek him. "

> *But without faith it is impossible to [walk with God and] please Him, for whoever comes [near] to God must [necessarily] believe that God exists and that He rewards those who [earnestly and diligently] seek Him. Hebrews 11:6 Amplified Bible (AMP)*

Revival Let It Rain

For righteous rain to fall there must be a person who earnestly seeks God, and who will receive what he teaches. Spiritual rain waters the seeds of the word of God planted in the hearts of people. God sends yarah, which may be teaching instruction, direction, or correction, or whatever one needs. A harvest of righteousness takes place in the person's life as a result. This benefits them, which in turn benefits those who receive encouragement or instruction from that person. This is how maturity comes to the one who turns to righteousness and others who enjoy a harvest from them. In the same way the earth must receive rain on a repeated basis, so those who walk with God must receive yarah throughout their days.

In the way an arrow is shot in a certain direction, it can rain in one place and not in another. Where we live, rain falls in one part of the city and not in another. Turn to righteousness, seek the Lord, and he will send the rain you've been waiting on.

> Revival Key #6 -. When one earnestly seeks the Lord, he sends revival rain. Just as wages are paid, the Lord rewards those who earnestly seek him. "

1. "G3406 - misthapodotēs - Strong's Greek Lexicon (KJV)." Blue Letter Bible. Web. 29 Mar, 2018. <https://www.blueletterbible.org//lang/lexicon/lexicon.cfm?Strongs=G3406&t=KJV>.

Chapter 10

Righteousness and Justice

5 The Lord loves righteousness and justice; the earth is full of his unfailing love. Psalm 33:5

Righteousness and justice need to be understood as the standard of God. Prophets throughout the Bible gave warnings when God's people strayed from righteousness. Hosea plainly told God's people, "But you have cultivated wickedness and harvested a thriving crop of sins" (Hosea 10:13a NLT). Job by experience also knew people got back according to kind. His example just as well uses the law of sowing and reaping.

8 My experience shows that those who plant trouble and cultivate evil will harvest the same. Job 4:8

Just as seed time and harvest function one then another, righteousness and justice work together as well. According to the Bible, righteousness and justice make up the foundation of God's throne. This sets the standards of the government of God.

"Clouds and thick darkness surround him; righteousness and justice are the foundation of his throne (Psalm 97:2).

Notice in the NIV Bible it says, "righteous and justice" but in the KJV Bible, "righteousness and judgment".

Clouds and darkness are round about him: righteousness and judgment are the habitation of his throne. Psalm 97:2 KJV

Righteousness in Psalms 97:2, tsedeq, is the same word as the second righteousness in Hosea 10:12. Tsedeq means "make right, to cleanse, clear self also to turn to righteousness, to be or do justice, justify; right (natural, moral or legal)."1 Judgment, mishpat, means "judgment, justice, and ordinance. It is used for the act of judging; act of deciding a case, a verdict (favorable or unfavorable)."2

Habitation, makown, is the "foundation or basis". 3 The" foundation of the throne of God is based on righteousness and judgment. 4 Isaiah prophesied of Jesus, who would reign on the throne of King David. His throne would be established "with justice and righteousness" (Isaiah 9:6-7). Without righteousness there would be no justice. When the righteousness of God does not reign, the justice of God goes to work to bring it. It is the justice or judgment of God that arises when correction is due. (Psalm 89:14, Psalm 9:7) Without God's standards of righteousness and justice operating, earth would be totally chaotic. Each person would do one's own thing and establish one's own standards of righteousness. (1 John 3:7-8)

As we see God requires righteousness and justice. The problem, sinful man cannot gain righteousness by works, no matter how hard we try. We needed help, so God sent his son Jesus to fulfill the requirement of righteousness to satisfy God's justice.

> 21 But now apart from the law the righteousness of God has been made known, to which the Law and the Prophets testify. 22 This righteousness is given through faith in Jesus Christ to all who believe. There is no difference between Jew and Gentile, 23 for all have sinned and fall short of the glory of God, 24 and all are justified freely by his grace through the redemption that came by Christ Jesus. 25 God presented Christ as a sacrifice of atonement, through the shedding of his blood—to be received by faith. He did this to demonstrate his righteousness, because in his forbearance he had left the sins committed beforehand unpunished— 26 he did it to demonstrate his righteousness at the present time, so as to be just and the one who justifies those who have faith in Jesus. Romans 3:21-26 NIV

Once righteousness and justice are established, then God's mercy flows. Hosea revealed this as well. Hosea pointed to the work of the cross when he called for righteousness which brought mercy.

> 4 But because of his great love for us, God, who is rich in mercy, 5 made us alive with Christ even when we were dead in transgressions—it is by grace you have been saved. 8 For it is by grace you have been saved, through faith—and this is not from yourselves, it is the gift of God— 9 not by works, so that no one can boast. Ephesians 2:4-5;8-9

God chose Abraham as the father of faith because he would train the next generation in righteousness and justice. As a result Abraham received all God promised him. As we train the next generation may we all reap the same benefits as Abraham.

Abraham was now very old, and the LORD had blessed him in every way. Genesis 24:1

> Revival Key #7 - God looks upon the individual who has turned to righteousness with his mercy. Then he requires a breaking up and away of what is in the way of fruitfulness. When done, now he rains upon them. This is not only what happens to an individual, but for the nation of the people. When God's people turn to righteousness, then their nation can reap the benefit of righteousness in government (judges and rulers). When he sends the rain, a harvest of righteousness, results in one's life.

1. "H6664 - tsedeq - Strong's Hebrew Lexicon (KJV)." Blue Letter Bible. Web. 31 Aug, 2016. <https://www.blueletterbible.org//lang/lexicon/lexicon.cfm?Strongs=H6664&t=KJV>.

2. "H4941 - mishpat - Strong's Hebrew Lexicon (KJV)." Blue Letter Bible. Web. 31 Aug, 2016. <https://www.blueletterbible.org//lang/lexicon/lexicon.cfm?Strongs=H4941&t=KJV>.

3. "H4349 - makown - Strong's Hebrew Lexicon (KJV)." Blue Letter Bible. Web. 31 Aug, 2016. <https://www.blueletterbible.org//lang/lexicon/lexicon.cfm?Strongs=H4349&t=KJV>.

4. Ibid.

Revival Let It Rain

Chapter 11

You Are the One

> *The Lord is far from the wicked but he hears the prayer of righteousness. Proverbs 15:29*

Abraham sat outside the entrance of his tent. What looked to be three men caught his sight. Abraham soon would realize the Lord was among them.

> *1The Lord appeared to Abraham near the great trees of Mamre while he was sitting at the entrance to his tent in the heat of the day. 2Abraham looked up and saw three men standing nearby. When he saw them, he hurried from the entrance of his tent to meet them and bowed low to the ground. Genesis 18*

At the close of their visit, the Lord began to reveal the pending judgment against the city of Sodom. Abraham stood in the gap by his prayer for the city.

> *16When the men got up to leave, they looked down toward Sodom, and Abraham walked along with them to see them on their way. 17Then the Lord said, "Shall I hide from Abraham what I am about to do? 18Abraham will surely become a great and powerful nation, and all nations on earth will be blessed through him. 19For I have chosen him, so that he will direct his children and his household after him to keep the way of the Lord by doing what is right and just, so that the Lord will bring about for Abraham what he has promised him." Genesis 18:16-19*

Abraham's nephew Lot lived in the area of pending judgment. So Abraham in respect pleaded for the city.

> *20 Then the Lord said, "The outcry against Sodom and Gomorrah is so great and their sin so grievous 21 that I will go down and see if what they have done is as bad as the outcry that has reached me. If not, I will know." 22 The men turned away and went toward Sodom, but Abraham remained standing before the Lord. 23 Then Abraham approached him and said: "Will you sweep away the righteous with the wicked? 24 What if there are fifty righteous people in the city? Will you really sweep it away and not spare the place for the sake of the fifty righteous people in it? 25 Far be it from you to do such a thing—to kill the righteous with the wicked, treating the righteous and the wicked alike. Far be it from you! Will not the Judge of all the earth do right?" Genesis 18:20-25*

Notice Abraham understood the righteousness of God. God promised not to destroy the city if righteous people were there.

> *26 The Lord said, "If I find fifty righteous people in the city of Sodom, I will spare the whole place for their sake." 27 Then Abraham spoke up again: "Now that I have been so bold as to speak to the Lord, though I am nothing but dust and ashes, 28 what if the number of the righteous is five less than fifty? Will you destroy the whole city for lack of five people?" "If I find forty-five there," he said, "I will not destroy it." 29 Once again he spoke to him, "What if only forty are found there?" He said, "For the sake of forty, I will not do it." 30 Then he said, "May the Lord not be angry, but let me speak. What if only thirty can be found there?" He answered, "I will not do it if I find thirty there." 31 Abraham said, "Now that I have been so bold as to speak to the Lord, what if only twenty can be found there?" He said, "For the sake of twenty, I will not destroy it." 32 Then he said, "May the Lord not be angry, but let me speak just once more. What if only ten can be found there?" He answered, "For the sake of ten, I will not destroy it." 33 When the Lord had finished speaking with Abraham, he left, and Abraham returned home. Genesis 18:26-32*

The sad thing about Sodom and Gomorrah was that ten righteous people were nonexistent in the area. So where did the outcry against the city come from? We know of no other possibility than Lot, Abraham's nephew. Could it be it was his outcry which brought God on the scene? Peter the apostle lets us know indeed it was Lot. Yes, the cry of one righteous person gets the ear of our righteous God. God listened to Abraham in Genesis 18:26-32, and he responded to Lot as well.

> *6 And turning the cities of Sodom and Gomorrah into ashes condemned [them] with an overthrow, making [them] an example unto those that after should live ungodly; 7 And delivered just Lot, vexed with the filthy conversation of the wicked: 8 (For that righteous man dwelling among them, in seeing and hearing, vexed [his] righteous soul from day to day with [their] unlawful deeds;) 9 The Lord knoweth how to deliver the godly out of temptations, and to reserve the unjust unto the day of judgment to be punished: 2 Peter 2:6-9 KJV*

Only Lot and his daughters escaped. Be in faith knowing God hears the righteous when they call out to him, including the injustice and wickedness about us.

Jeremiah the prophet received a command from the Lord to look for just one person in Jerusalem who sought the truth and dealt honesty. If Jeremiah could find this one person, God promised to forgive the entire city.

> *1 "Go up and down the streets of Jerusalem, look around and consider, search through her squares. If you can find but one person who deals honestly and seeks the truth, I will forgive this city. 2Although they say, 'As surely as the Lord lives,' still they are swearing falsely." 3Lord, do not your eyes look for truth? You struck them, but they felt no pain; you crushed them, but they refused correction. They made their faces harder than stone and refused to repent. Jeremiah 5:1 NIV*

Jeremiah looked, but not even one person who fit the required description could be found. The people used religious talk but continued to lie. So the city and its people came under God's judgment. The Lord approached Ezekiel 22:30 with the same type of request. Ezekiel had the same problem as did Jeremiah: he could find none.

> *23Again a message came to me from the LORD: 24"Son of man, give the people of Israel this message: In the day of my indignation, you will be like a polluted land, a land without rain. 25Your princes plot conspiracies just as lions stalk their prey. They devour innocent people, seizing treasures and extorting wealth. They make many widows in the land. 26Your priests have violated my instructions and defiled my holy things. They make no*

> *distinction between what is holy and what is not. And they do not teach my people the difference between what is ceremonially clean and unclean. They disregard my Sabbath days so that I am dishonored among them. 27Your leaders are like wolves who tear apart their victims. They actually destroy people's lives for money! 28And your prophets cover up for them by announcing false visions and making lying predictions. They say, 'My message is from the Sovereign LORD,' when the LORD hasn't spoken a single word to them. 29Even common people oppress the poor, rob the needy, and deprive foreigners of justice."* **I looked for someone who might rebuild the wall of righteousness that guards the land.** *I searched for someone to stand in the gap in the wall so I wouldn't have to destroy the land, but I found no one. Ezekiel 22:23-30 NLT*

Why was it so important to find just one person? Remember righteousness and justice established the throne of God's kingdom (Psalm 92:7). It cannot be established on anything else.

One person can "rebuild the wall of righteousness that guards a land" (Ezekiel 22:30). To find just one person who walked in righteousness would give God a person to work with in the land. God did this with Enoch, Noah, and Abraham in their day. All three men walked with God among many who did not. Without righteousness and justice, the government of God cannot be established.

Let's expand this principal; God needs just one person in any area of life to build a wall of righteousness. Do not think one's prayers and walk with the Lord is insignificant.

> *The prayer of a righteous person is powerful and effective.* James 5:16b

For a moment let's think about something. God told both Jeremiah and Ezekiel to look for one righteous person to stop pending judgment. None was found. In the case of Sodom and Gomorrah, there was one righteous person living there. God did not ask Abraham to look for a righteous man to spare the city. Why? The one righteous man left could not handle being there anymore. I will use the Amplified Bible to expand how Lot felt.

> *Lot, who was tormented by the immoral conduct of unprincipled and ungodly men 8 (for that just man, while living among them, felt his righteous soul tormented day after day by what he saw and heard of their lawless acts),* 2 Peter 2:7-8 AMP

Tormented by what he endured in Sodom and Gomorrah, Lot cried out to God. God heard him and decided to come down and check things out. Now God knows all things. Why would God come down to see (Genesis 18:20-21)? God would rather people turn from sin and live.

> *"Do you think that I like to see wicked people die? says the Sovereign LORD. Of course not! I want them to turn from their wicked ways and live. Ezekiel 18:23 NLT*

Nevertheless, when the wicked will not turn from their evil ways, God will "keep them under punishment until the day of judgment" (2 Peter 2:5). For the righteous, God will rescue them from their tormentors.

And yet another prophet Daniel stood in the gap for the restoration of Jerusalem. Daniel understood the times in which he lived by reading the Word of God. He discovered Jeremiah's word of seventy years. From this Daniel understood Jerusalem desolations neared its end. Daniel "confessed his sins and the sins of his people" (Daniel 9:20). One righteous person stood in the gap. The result was God sent the angel Gabriel to give him the understanding he needed. God sent the rain that changed a nation.

Revival Let It Rain

Chapter 12

National Revival

With the completion of the Lord's temple, King Solomon and all Israel celebrated. The king lifted up his hands to heaven and prayed.

> *12Then Solomon stood before the altar of the LORD in front of the whole assembly of Israel and spread out his hands. 14He said: "LORD, the God of Israel, there is no God like you in heaven or on earth—you who keep your covenant of love with your servants who continue wholeheartedly in your way. 15You have kept your promise to your servant David my father; with your mouth you have promised and with your hand you have fulfilled it—as it is today. 2 Chronicles 6:12; 14-15*

King Solomon entered into intercession for Israel, a people he knew fell into sin. Solomon also understood people who acknowledged and repented of their sin would receive God's mercy. In 2 Chronicles chapter 6, Solomon's intercession dealt with various scenarios of God's judgment. According to the foundation of God's throne, when unrighteousness arises, God's justice issues a judgment. The goal is to turn a person or a nation back to righteousness.

> *24"When your people Israel have been defeated by an enemy because they have sinned against you and when they turn back and give praise to your name, praying and making supplication before you in this temple, 25then hear from heaven and forgive the sin of your people Israel and bring them back to the land you gave to them and their ancestors. 26"When the heavens are shut up and there is no rain because your people have sinned against you, and when they pray toward this place and give praise to your name and turn from their sin because you have afflicted*

> them, 27then hear from heaven and forgive the sin of your servants, your people Israel. Teach them the right way to live, and send rain on the land you gave your people for an inheritance. 28"When famine or plague comes to the land, or blight or mildew, locusts or grasshoppers, or when enemies besiege them in any of their cities, whatever disaster or disease may come, 29and when a prayer or plea is made by anyone among your people Israel—being aware of their afflictions and pains, and spreading out their hands toward this temple— 30then hear from heaven, your dwelling place. Forgive, and deal with everyone according to all they do, since you know their hearts (for you alone know the human heart),31so that they will fear you and walk in obedience to you all the time they live in the land you gave our ancestors. 2 Chronicles 6:24-31 NIV

After the king finished he returned to his palace. Then during the night the Lord came to Solomon. The Lord recites back to King Solomon judgments that arise against a people. This assured King Solomon that indeed the Lord heard his prayer.

> 12the Lord appeared to him at night and said: "I have heard your prayer and have chosen this place for myself as a temple for sacrifices. 13"When I shut up the heavens so that there is no rain, or command locusts to devour the land or send a plague among my people ... 2 Chronicles 7:12-13

God knows some people praise and worship him one day and turn away the next. So he issued the prescription for this behavior.

> 14if my people, who are called by my name, will humble themselves and pray and seek my face and turn from their wicked ways, then I will hear from heaven, and I will forgive their sin and will heal their land. 2 Chronicles 7:14

A merciful God clearly reveals how to turn a person and a nation from rebellion back to him. Not everybody can do this, but only those who are called by the name of the Lord. The prescription for turning a nation to the Lord begins with an individual. Then others can come aboard.

1) Take off one's pride and humble oneself before the Lord.

2) Pray and seek God.

3) Turn from ones wicked ways.

When one takes these steps, the Lord states: "… then I will hear from heaven, and I will forgive their sin and will heal their land. " (2 Chronicles 7:14).

> Revival Key #8 – Intercession - Stand in the gap as did Daniel. Pray for one's region (city, county, state, and nation). As the righteous people of God, stand on his word for our nation. He is faithful and just to watch his word to perform it.

When God wants to do something in a place, he looks for one righteousness person. If he can't find one, he'll look for someone to draw to him. If he cannot do this, there will be continued problems in the land.

> *44 No man can come to me, except the Father which hath sent me draw him: and I will raise him up at the last day. John 6:44 KJV*

If one person will respond to God by turning to righteousness, then he has a foundation to work from in one's life and in one's nation. 2 Chronicles 7:14 proves to be an absolute amazing promise from the Lord. He listens when the righteous call out to him. He will pardon their sins and restore their land. Hosea 10:12 spoke the same remedy for the path of restoration.

> Revival Key #9 - "Pray in the Spirit at all times and on every occasion. Stay alert and be persistent in your prayers for all believers everywhere" (Ephesians 6:18). "For if I pray in a tongue, my spirit prays, but my mind is unfruitful. 15So what shall I do? I will pray with my spirit, but I will also pray with my understanding;   1 Corinthians 14:14

Revival Let It Rain

Chapter 13

The Cycle of Work and Rest

We all understand our bodies require times of inactivity. We know God set sleep as a part of our daily cycle. This cycle began when God placed the sun and the moon in orbit on the fourth day of creation (Genesis 1:14-19). Cycles that evolve around the sun and moon govern our lives. When one thinks about creation with all its details, God's awesomeness surely shines. "The heavens declare the glory of God, and the sky above proclaims his handiwork" (Psalm 19:1 English Standard Version).

In our lives it takes work of some kind to get things done. Adam found out how hard working the land could be after he and Eve disobeyed God. Not only did Eve's pain increase in childbirth, Adam's labor became painful as well.

> *17 To Adam he said, "Because you listened to your wife and ate fruit from the tree about which I commanded you, 'You must not eat from it,' Cursed is the ground because of you; through painful toil you will eat food from it all the days of your life. Genesis 3:17*

> *... cursed is the ground for thy sake; in sorrow shalt thou eat of it all the days of thy life; Genesis 3:17 KJV*

From the King James Bible, the word sorrow "itstsabown" describes "pain, labor and hardship." 2 In Genesis 5:2 a patriarch Lamech had this in mind when he named his son Noah. Noah's name just happened to mean "rest." The gist from the New Living Translation: Lamech prayed that Noah would bring relief from the painful labor of farming (Genesis 5:29).

> *29Lamech named his son Noah, for he said, "May he bring us relief from our work and the painful labor of farming this ground that the LORD has cursed." Genesis 5 29 NLT*

When anyone called to Noah, they were essentially calling forth rest. From the New American Standard Bible, we discover Lamech also gave Noah his name by prophetic inspiration. "Now he called his name Noah, saying, "This one will give us rest from our work and from the toil of our hands arising from the ground which the LORD has cursed" (Genesis 5:29 NASB).

Lamech's prophetic insight proved to be true. Through obedience to God's command, Noah and his family gained rest that none other in his generation received.

> *5 And spared not the old world, but saved Noah the eighth [person], a preacher of righteousness, bringing in the flood upon the world of the ungodly; 2 Peter 2:4-5 KJV*

The first one to enjoy rest in the Bible was none other than God himself. Shabath, the Hebrew word for rest found in Genesis 2:2, means "to cease, desist and rest." 3

> *2And on the seventh day God ended his work which he had made; and he rested on the seventh day from all his work which he had made. 3And God blessed the seventh day, and sanctified it: because that in it he had rested from all his work which God created and made. Genesis 2:2-3 KJV*

When God finished his work, he rested. Furthermore, God set apart a Sabbath day rest for Israel, and he "made it holy" (Genesis 2:3). The Sabbath day reminded Israel that God himself rested from his work. Jesus revealed its purpose as well in the New Testament. "The Sabbath was made for man, not man for the Sabbath" (Mark 2:27).

Exodus 23 explains God's commandments to Israel concerning rest for their land and people. Whatever the land produced during the seventh year became food for the poor. "You shall sow your land six years and harvest its yield, 11 but the seventh year you shall let it rest and lie uncultivated, so that the poor among your people may eat [what the land grows naturally]; whatever they leave the animals of the field may eat. You shall do the same with your vineyard and olive grove" (Exodus 23:10-12 Amplified Bible).

Not only do humans and land need a period of rest, so do animals. From the New International Bible, this point stands out.

> *12"Six days do your work, but on the seventh day do not work, so that your ox and your donkey may rest, and so that the slave born in your household and the foreigner living among you may be refreshed." Exodus 23:12*

We want to make sure there is a time to rest. On the other hand, what happens if someone will not work? Then the cycle which brings benefit from work does not occur. "How long will you lie there, you sluggard? When will you get up from your sleep? A little sleep, a little slumber, a little folding of the hands to rest--and poverty will come on you like a thief and scarcity like an armed man" (Proverbs 6:9-11).

As we know sowing, reaping, seasons, days, and years are all cycles of repetition. Rest and work are as well. During the night cycle as creation rests, it prepares for the coming of the sun and the work cycle. I know some have jobs at night and sleep during the day, but in itself it is a cycle of work and rest. At nighttime even plants prepare for daytime. Earth cycles work together to bring needed correction. For example, during the winter season, freezing weather kills off pesky insects. This corrects overpopulation of the summer months. It is obvious God placed in creation these cycles with purpose. To understand more of their significance, we look at a process called circadian rhythms.

> *"Circadian rhythms are a daily cycle of biological activity based on a 24-hour period and influenced by regular variations in the environment, such as the alternation of night and day. Circadian rhythms include sleeping and waking of animals, flower closing and opening in angiosperms, and tissue growth and differentiation in fungi. "The circadian rhythm, present in humans and most animals, is generated by an internal clock that is synchronized to light-dark cycles and other cues in organism's environment. This internal clock accounts for waking up at the same time every day even without an alarm clock. It also causes nocturnal animals to function at night when diurnal creatures are at rest. Circadian rhythms can be disrupted by changes in daily schedule. Biologists have observed that birds exposed to artificial light for a long time sometimes build nests in the fall instead of the spring." 1-1*

> *"Circadian rhythms are also important in determining human sleep patterns. The body's master clock, or SCN, controls the production of melatonin, a hormone that makes you sleepy. Since it is located just above the optic nerves, which relay information from the eyes to the brain, the SCN receives information about incoming light. When there is less light—like at night—the SCN tells the brain to make more melatonin so you get drowsy."* 4

When we sleep, we rest. Long periods of time without sleep can make us physically ill. I can attest to this, especially on a trip we took many years ago. My husband and I thought it would be great to drive down to the coast for a weekend. Off we went, driving most of the day until late that night. But it was Labor Day weekend, and we could not find a room for the night anywhere. I mean nowhere. So my husband and I watched the sunrise, got some breakfast and started driving north. One of us drove as the other took a cat nap. Talk about tired. We were queasy and so worn out. We needed some serious sleep. About an hour north from the coast, we finally found a room. Both of us slept for hours without any movement. Sleep is so good when one gets it. Without sleep, it is rough. Rest provides our bodies time to be restored physically, mentally, and spiritually. Just as nutrients restore to land that rests, our bodies enjoy this process as we heal from our labor. Rest enables God to prepare us for what's next.

Chapter 14

Restoration in His Presence

Just as cycles exist in our physical world, cycles are at work in our walk with God. Jesus took time to get away from activity. His purpose remained clear: to get into the presence of his Father and pray (Luke 5:16).

He withdrew to places where it was just him and the father God. Jesus did this not once or twice but regularly. "After he had dismissed them, he went up on a mountainside by himself to pray. Later that night, he was there alone" (Matthew 14:23).

Jesus cultivated a relationship with the Father. He required alone time with him. During these times, Jesus did not teach multitudes or heal the sick. .

> *32That evening after sunset the people brought to Jesus all the sick and demon-possessed. 33The whole town gathered at the door,34and Jesus healed many who had various diseases. He also drove out many demons, but he would not let the demons speak because they knew who he was. 35Very early in the morning, while it was still dark, Jesus got up, left the house and went off to a solitary place, where he prayed.36Simon and his companions went to look for him, 37and when they found him, they exclaimed "Everyone is looking for you!":38Jesus replied, "Let us go somewhere else—to the nearby villages—so I can preach there also. That is why I have come." 39So he traveled throughout Galilee, preaching in their synagogues and driving out demons. Mark 1:32-39*

While in prayer Jesus received instruction on where he would go next. He needed to move on and preach to other towns as well. Notice the statement when his disciples found him: "Everyone is looking for you!" (Mark 1:37). The demand of people did not sway Jesus to disobey the Father. Nor did others who attempted to keep Jesus with them in Luke 4:42. When Jesus prayed and heard from the father, he did what he was told.

> *42At daybreak, Jesus went out to a solitary place. The people were looking for him and when they came to where he was, they tried to keep him from leaving them. 43But he said, "I must proclaim the good news of the kingdom of God to the other towns also, because that is why I was sent." Luke 4:42-43*

On another occasion he came out of prayer and called twelve men to himself. Out of all his disciples, these 12 would be his apostles (Luke 6:12-13). If Jesus required time to get alone with the Father and pray, so do we all. This is what it takes to prepare for our own destinies. There must be time alone with the Lord for fellowship and prayer. There one must listen for God's plan in order to carry out one's assignment. This propels us into our destinies.

Important decisions came when Jesus withdrew to pray. His confidence stood strong as he heard from the Father. Seeking the Father in prayer brought the yarah rain he needed. Jesus came out with focus to press on to fulfill his own God given destiny. He came out readied for what was next in his life and ministry.

Just as people need to sleep, another type of rest exists for the weary. This important benefit comes from spending time with the Lord. He will give you rest for one's soul. Restoration occurs in the presence of God.

> *28"Come to me, all you who are weary and burdened, and I will give you rest. 29 Take my yoke upon you and learn from me, for I am gentle and humble in heart, and you will find rest for your souls. Matthew 11:28-29*

I like the way the Message Bible reads for Matthew 11:28-29. This type of rest can only be provided by the Lord.

> *28-30 "Are you tired? Worn out? Burned out on religion? Come to me. Get away with me and you'll recover your life. I'll show you how to take a real rest. Walk with me and work with me—watch how I do it. Learn the unforced rhythms of grace. I won't lay anything heavy or ill-fitting on you. Keep company with me*

and you'll learn to live freely and lightly." Matthew 11:28-29 Message Bible.

Jesus will show anyone who asks how to enter into his rest. The Greek word for rest anapauō means "1) to cause or permit one to cease from any movement or labor in order to recover and collect his strength; 2) to give rest, refresh, to give one's self rest, take rest."1

,... "Come with me by yourselves to a quiet place and get some rest." Mark 6:31

Does the reader need rest? Are you tired, worn out, or burned out? Jesus invites you to come away with him. May the Lord teach us how to live our lives through his grace as he imparts rest for our weary bodies and souls.

> Revival Key #10 – Get in the Presence of God daily. Allow ones love relationship with him to flourish. Make sure to hear and follow his instructions.

1. "G373 - anapauō - Strong's Greek Lexicon (KJV)." Blue Letter Bible. Web. 11 Oct, 2016. <https://www.blueletterbible.org//lang/lexicon/lexicon.cfm?Strongs=G373&t=KJV>.

Revival Let It Rain

Chapter 15

Waking Up Dormant Ground

For everything there is a season, a time for every activity under heaven. Ecclesiastes 3:1

Recall fallow ground is land set aside for a period of rest. The word dormant describes what's going on with fallow ground. Dormant means "lying asleep or as if a sleep; in a state of rest or inactivity."1 When God tells a person to break up one's fallow ground, it indicates there's vision in one's heart lying in a dormant state. Fallow ground represents a dormant or a rest cycle in operation. Something in the plan of God for one's life must now awake.

A person's God ordained destiny is known by God before one's conception. The Bible's reveals God's vision and purpose for earth through mankind. God worked through many in the Bible who were given visions from him to walk out. Jeremiah, the prophet understood this truth from the Lord.

"Before I formed you in the womb I knew you, before you were born I set you apart; I appointed you as a prophet to the nations." Jeremiah 1:5

Upon turning to righteousness, God reveals the end from the beginning as he unfolds a vision for one's life. Jeremiah did not understand his call as a prophet to the nations until God revealed it to him. Realizing fulfillment of one's vision from God will take place on God's timetable and not ours. Not all aspects of one's life vision will come to pass at once either. For example, even if a child dreams of marrying, that cannot take place until adulthood.

God given dreams and visions will sit on fallow ground in one's heart until an appointed time. When God begins to awaken a part of a person's vision, that particular aspect will begin to revive. Take Adam, for instance. He walked in a part of his destiny while other areas lay dormant and unfulfilled. Adam named all the animals and living creatures. He realized all he named consisted of both a male and female, but he found no female like himself.

> *20 And Adam gave names to all cattle, and to the fowl of the air, and to every beast of the field; but for Adam there was not found a help meet for him. Genesis 2:20 KJV*

Adam's ability to multiply like kind of himself remained dormant. It merely was a word from God at this point.

> *27So God created mankind in his own image, in the image of God he created them; male and female he created them. 28God blessed them and said to them, "Be fruitful and increase in number; fill the earth and subdue it. Rule over the fish in the sea and the birds in the sky and over every living creature that moves on the ground." Genesis 1:27-28*

In Genesis 1:27-28 God gave us a snapshot of his mandate for mankind. For Adam this remained impossible at this point in his life. The ingredient to fulfill multiplication remained missing. This part of Adam's life's destiny lay dormant. If God didn't work to bring the necessary change, Adam's destiny would remain unfulfilled. Interestingly, the first use of sleep in the Bible prepared Adam for destiny. God induced Adam into a deep sleep.

> *So the LORD God caused the man to fall into a deep sleep; and while he was sleeping, he took one of the man's ribs and then closed up the place with flesh. Genesis 2:21*

God used sleep to work on Adam's life. He readied Adam for multiplication. Think about this. Adam's destiny could not be fulfilled prior to God's intervention. During this sleep, Adam remained unconscious and unaware of what God accomplished. Similarly while a patient sleeps, a surgeon does needed correction. Not until one awakes does a patient become aware of the results. This happened with Adam. Not until he became conscious did God reveal Eve. God made ready the next chapter of his destiny. Also Adam could not fulfill his God given purpose alone. God likewise prepared another person to be readied who changed Adam's life. Together they would fulfill God given destiny and purpose.

Another factor of sleep is that God gives us dreams and visions as we slumber. Through these God warns, teaches, directs, or whatever he deems necessary for the recipient. "For God speaks again and again, though people do not recognize it. 15He speaks in dreams, in visions of the night, when deep sleep falls on people as they lie in their beds. 16He whispers in their ears and terrifies them with warnings. 17He makes them turn from doing wrong; he keeps them from pride. 18He protects them from the grave, from crossing over the river of death" (Job 33:14-18) NLT.

God has also given promises to a person that sometimes will not be fulfilled until a future generation. This factor may be at work in our destinies. The Lord revealed to a childless man that his descendants would be in bondage for 400 years. This again shows God revealing the end from the beginning of one's destiny.

> *1After this, the word of the Lord came to Abram in a vision: "Do not be afraid, Abram. I am your shield, your very great reward." 2But Abram said, "Sovereign Lord, what can you give me since I remain childless and the one who will inherit my estate is Eliezer of Damascus?" 3And Abram said, "You have given me no children; so a servant in my household will be my heir." 4Then the word of the Lord came to him: "This man will not be your heir, but a son who is your own flesh and blood will be your heir." 5He took him outside and said, "Look up at the sky and count the stars—if indeed you can count them." Then he said to him, "So shall your offspring be." 6Abram believed the Lord, and he credited it to him as righteousness. 7He also said to him, "I am the Lord, who brought you out of Ur of the Chaldeans to give you this land to take possession of it." Genesis 15:1-7*

Abram cried out to God for a son as he and Sarah remained childless. Although Abram knew the promise, that particular part of Abram's vision remained in dormancy. Not until a period of time according to God's timing did the birth of Isaac occur. In such a case, God waits for his timing, not ours, to bring fulfillment. Sometimes it takes a long time to get to a point of fulfillment. We end up putting it out of our mind or give up all together.

I can give the reader an example from my life. God spoke to me that we would have children, but it took years and years before fulfillment. That part of God's plan for my life lay dormant. Not until God's appointed time did he approach me to stir up my faith once again. Then I needed to break away every weed and remove every rock I allowed in my heart. What do these look like? Anything that brought doubt, unbelief, disappointment, or disillusionment had to go. Such thoughts insisted I give up this dream. No longer could that ground in my heart remain dormant. God came with the water of his word which began the process to revive the dream.

This happened to Sarah as well. She laughed when the Lord said she would have a child. She looked at her age and the impossibility of that dream ever coming to pass. Nonetheless, when it came time to give Abraham and Sarah a son, the Lord came to them. He came with a promise. The time came for them to wake up this dormant part of their life's vision.

> *9"Where is your wife Sarah?" they asked him. "There, in the tent," he said. 10Then one of them said, "I will surely return to you about this time next year, and Sarah your wife will have a son." Now Sarah was listening at the entrance to the tent, which was behind him. 11Abraham and Sarah were already very old, and Sarah was past the age of childbearing. 12So Sarah laughed to herself as she thought, "After I am worn out and my lord is old, will I now have this pleasure?" 13Then the Lord said to Abraham, "Why did Sarah laugh and say, 'Will I really have a child, now that I am old?' 14Is anything too hard for the Lord? I will return to you at the appointed time next year, and Sarah will have a son." Genesis 18:9-14*

Abraham needed God to show up in his life in a mighty way for any promise to come to pass. The Lord came to revive the vision. God not only promised him a son but spoke of countless descendants coming from him.

> *12As the sun was setting, Abram fell into a deep sleep, and a thick and dreadful darkness came over him. 13Then the Lord said to him, "Know for certain that for four hundred years your descendants will be strangers in a country not their own and that they will be enslaved and mistreated there. 14But I will punish the nation they serve as slaves, and afterward they will come out with great possessions. 15You, however, will go to your ancestors in peace and be buried at a good old age. 16In the fourth generation your descendants will come back here, for the sin of the Amorites has not yet reached its full measure." Genesis 15:12-16*

Vickie Bryan

Chapter 16

An Appointed Time

Abraham's family's vision was set for fulfillment at an appointed time. Not until exactly 430 years did God free Abraham's descendants from bondage. The book of Exodus records when God fulfilled this prophetic word to Abraham hundreds of years later. It is amazing how this actually worked out.

> *40Now the length of time the Israelite people lived in Egypt was 430 years. 41At the end of the 430 years, to the very day, all the Lord's divisions left Egypt. Exodus 12:40-41*

People in Abraham's family line fulfilled different parts of the vision spoken to him. One of them ended up in prison on a false charge. Joseph's destiny would preserve Abraham's family line through famine. Ironically this famine also sent Jacob and his family to Egypt, where his descendants eventually would end up in slavery.

God gave Joseph dreams of his life's destiny as a youth. Because his father favored him above the rest of his brothers, the dream did not set well will them.

> *1Jacob lived in the land where his father had stayed, the land of Canaan. 2This is the account of Jacob's family line. Joseph, a young man of seventeen, was tending the flocks with his brothers, the sons of Bilhahand the sons of Zilpah, his father's wives, and he brought their father a bad report about them. 3Now Israel loved Joseph more than any of his other sons, because he had been born to him in his old age; and he made an ornate robe for him. 4When his brothers saw that their father loved him more than any of them, they hated him and could not speak a kind word to him. 5Joseph had a dream, and when he told it to his*

61

> *brothers, they hated him all the more. 6He said to them, "Listen to this dream I had:7We were binding sheaves of grain out in the field when suddenly my sheaf rose and stood upright, while your sheaves gathered around mine and bowed down to it." 8His brothers said to him, "Do you intend to reign over us? Will you actually rule us?" And they hated him all the more because of his dream and what he had said. 9Then he had another dream, and he told it to his brothers. "Listen," he said, "I had another dream, and this time the sun and moon and eleven stars were bowing down to me." 10When he told his father as well as his brothers, his father rebuked him and said, "What is this dream you had? Will your mother and I and your brothers actually come and bow down to the ground before you?" 11His brothers were jealous of him, but his father kept the matter in mind.* Genesis 37:1-11

As a result jealousy arose as Joseph was sold into slavery where he ended up in Egypt. Joseph had been gifted by God to interpret dreams. While in prison year after year, time ticked away. How could Joseph's dream get out of prison? It lay dormant in his heart as he waited for an appointed time. God needed Joseph, and sure enough God began to move on Joseph's behalf. He was delivered out of prison to Pharaoh. What did God use to get Joseph out? The gift of interpreting dreams made the way for Joseph to step into his destiny. This was none other than the anointing of God on Joseph's life. He became second in command of the entire nation of Egypt.

> *You will arise and have compassion on Zion, for it is time to show favor to her; the appointed time has come.* Psalm 102:13

Joseph's God given dream sat in a dormant state. Just as he became bound by slavery, so did his vision from God. It seemed impossible as Joseph and his dream remained imprisoned. His God given dream slept inside his heart. It laid there inactive. All through whatever came Joseph's way, God's favor rested on him. This provided Joseph the opportunity to be trained and readied when the time came. Even in tough situations, God prepared his man. Did Joseph give up due to his circumstances? I bet he thought about it. Something deep inside would not let go of the dream. God began to move on his behalf. Revival headed his way. His break came when two men were sent to prison, each with dreams, and the need for interpretation arose. Joseph's opportunity came, and he stepped through the door. God did everything as he revealed to Joseph as a youth. His early vision and dreams did not give every little detail of all that would happen to him. No, these required an ongoing relationship with God to get through, but on the way he was being readied for destiny. (Genesis 37-47)

Joseph's destiny waited for an appointed time. God did not change his mind, and he brought it to pass. Do not give up on one's dream.

> *3 For the vision [is] yet for an appointed time, but at the end it shall speak, and not lie: though it tarry, wait for it; because it will surely come, it will not tarry. Habakkuk 2:3 KJV*

Revival Let It Rain

Chapter 17

A Promise to Revive

> *Blessed is the nation whose God is the Lord, the people he chose for his inheritance. Psalm 33:12*

We know wrongdoing had prevailed, and people needed to repent in order to change their nation. From Jeremiah, just as Hosea, Judah and Jerusalem clearly heard what the Lord required of them.

> *1 "O Israel," says the LORD, "if you wanted to return to me, you could. You could throw away your detestable idols and stray away no more. 2 Then when you swear by my name, saying, 'As surely as the LORD lives,' you could do so with truth, justice, and righteousness. Then you would be a blessing to the nations of the world, and all people would come and praise my name." 3 This is what the LORD says to the people of Judah and Jerusalem: "Plow up the hard ground of your hearts! Do not waste your good seed among thorns. 4 O people of Judah and Jerusalem, surrender your pride and power. Change your hearts before the LORD, or my anger will burn like an unquenchable fire because of all your sins. and all people would come and praise my name."*
> *Jeremiah 4:1-4 NLT*

How does one turn to the Lord? The same way Hosea revealed: by turning to righteousness. If one knows the Lord, live like it in "truth, justice, and righteousness" (Jeremiah 4:2). Isaiah 57:15 contains God's promise to revive his people. One must come to him with a humble and repentant spirit. Then he promises to "revive the spirit of the humble, and to revive the heart of the contrite" (Isaiah 57:15). Furthermore God provides grace to the humble. (James 4:4-6).

> *For thus saith the high and lofty One that inhabiteth eternity, whose name is Holy; I dwell in the high and holy place, with him also that is of a contrite and humble spirit, to revive the spirit of the humble, and to revive the heart of the contrite ones.*
> *Isaiah 57:15 KJV*

God will restore one's crushed spirit. Then he revives one's courage. The opposite of courage is fear, and fear shuts down faith. With one's spirit and courage restored, then one will be ready to walk out the plan of God in righteousness. According to Jeremiah 4:2, when God's people walked in righteousness, "they would be a blessing to the nations of the world." Then "all people would come and praise my name" (Jeremiah 4:2). In this way righteousness brings revival and God gets his glory.

Chapter 18

Restoration

Hosea's message to Israel was clear: God desired their restoration. To the believers reading this book, it only takes one righteous person to change a nation. It only takes one person to follow the prescription laid out in this book to bring change to one's life and those around you.

As a believer, it takes an ongoing walk with the Lord to finish our race well. Sometimes we falter and get off track. Sin creeps in as our faith weakens. One does not need to stay there. Draw near to God, and he will draw near to you. He is calling the reader to his side. The Lord will replenish and restore what the enemy has stolen. If that fits the reader, let's pray.

> *Heavenly Father, I realize I am not where I need to be in my walk with you. I have allowed _____ to weaken my faith. I ask you to forgive me of _____. Replenish and restore me in every way. I want to know your love even more. I want to fulfill the divine purpose you planned for my life. Take charge of my life and lead me to fulfill that purpose. I want to hear you say to me one day, "Well done my good and faithful servant" (Matthew 25:21)* 1

Receive the Lord and his restoration of one's dreams with joy. When one finds rest in Jesus, one never wants to leave his presence. A walk with him will be an ongoing love relationship. The Lord changed forever a man who had been bound by the devil. Read his desire to stay close to him. Then read what Jesus told him to do. Go and do likewise.

As Jesus was getting into the boat, the demon-delivered man begged to go along, but he wouldn't let him. Jesus said, "Go home to your own people. Tell them your story—what the Master did, how he had mercy on you." The man went back and began to preach in the Ten Towns area about what Jesus had done for him. He was the talk of the town. Mark 5: 18-20 The Message (MSG)

Chapter 19

The Former and Latter Rain

Joel, another Old Testament prophet, spoke of the rain. He lived in Judah over a hundred years before the time of Hosea. Joel used the same terminology of "the former and latter rain" as did Hosea.

23 Be glad then, ye children of Zion, and rejoice in the LORD your God: for he hath given you the former rain moderately, and he will cause to come down for you the rain, the former rain, and the latter rain in the first [month]. Joel 2:23 (KJV)

Did the reader notice the word "rain" appears four times in this scripture? One would think the same Hebrew word would be in use. Only two of them meet this criterion. Below the appropriate Hebrew word is adjacent to each "rain" in the verse.

Be glad then, ye children of Zion, and rejoice in the LORD your God: for he hath given you the former rain (mowreh) moderately, and he will cause to come down for you the rain (geshem) the former rain, (mowreh) and the latter rain (malqowsh) the first month. 5 Joel 2:23 KJV

The first rain mowreh in Joel 2:23 describes the "(early) rain".1 Mowreh additionally denotes "a teacher such as God or a prophet" and a shooter, darter or archer."2 This sounds like yarah rain. Upon inspection mowreh is a root word of yarah and it makes up the subject of Joel's prophesy.3

In Joel 2:23, God gave the former or early rain mowreh moderately. Moderately tsĕdaqah in Joel 2:23 revealed how the rain came. "The early rain came according to right."4 This meant the rain was not a flood, but the right amount.

The first rain mowreh occurred three times in scripture. It was used twice in Joel 2:23 and once in Psalms 84:6.

> Who passing through the valley of Baca make it a well; the rain also filleth the pools. Psalms 84:6 KJV

What does "passing through the valley of Baca" have to do with anything (Psalms 84:6)? A little side step here will be worth it.

Valley emeq means "low lands" or a "broad depression."5 Another meaning for valley is "any place, period, or situation that is filled with fear, gloom, foreboding, or the like."6 This fits as Baca in Hebrew is "a valley of "weeping, lamentation."7 In one way, "valley of Baca" can be thought of as depression, a low in one's life. Sometimes people go through tough times resulting in such a state. This can come in many situations in a lifetime including the process of fulfilling one's life's dreams.

The Hebrew word `emeq (Strong's H6010) valley "is a low tract of land, of wide extent, fit for corn and suited for battle fields."8 In plural emeg appears to be once used for the inhabitants of valleys. In 1 Chronicles 12:15, the Gadites put to "flight all the inhabitants of valleys but perhaps it should read "all the Anakim." 9

> 14These Gadites were army commanders; the least was a match for a hundred, and the greatest for a thousand. 15It was they who crossed the Jordan in the first month when it was overflowing all its banks, and they put to flight everyone living in the valleys, to the east and to the west. 1 Chronicles 12:14-15

Anakims were a "long-necked, a tribe of giants, descendants of Anak, which dwelled in southern Canaan."10 I have written on the subject of giants from the Bible. *Living with the Nephilim, the Seed of Destruction* will provide any reader a greater understanding of the subject. Also "emeq was used for the valley of the Rephaim from Joshua 15:8, 18:16."11

> ... and the border went up to the top of the mountain that lieth before the valley of Hinnom westward, which is at the end of the valley of the giants northward: Joshua 15:8b KJV

Rephaim happens to be another race of giants. Giants or Nephilim practiced false religions, idolatry, sorcery/witchcraft and the like which God always opposes. This type of behavior releases demonic activity from the spirit realm. The valley of Baca may represent a spiritual attack. Anytime God has a plan and a purpose for anyone, Satan will oppose it. Israel's warriors, the Gadites, fought to remove the enemy from their promised land. Similarly, we must do spiritual warfare against any enemy seeking to hinder us, including depression and lamentation. We are not to continue in this condition as children of the Most High God. Why? We have a promise that he will send the rain.

Look how God turns this around in Psalms 84:6. He makes the valley a well. This is a fountain of rain. "When they walk through the Valley of Weeping, it will become a place of refreshing springs. The autumn rains will clothe it with blessings" (Psalms 84:6 NLT).

This "spring becomes a source (of satisfaction").12 The rain not only becomes a well, but a fountain. God takes one from sorrow to a place of blessing. This is such a glorious promise.

> *5How blessed is the man whose strength is in You, In whose heart are the highways to Zion! 6Passing through the valley of Baca they make it a spring; The early rain also covers it with blessings.7They go from strength to strength, Every one of them appears before God in Zion. Psalms 84:4-7 NASB*

Now back to Joel 2:23 and the second rain, (H1653). Geshem means, "rain, shower, also a violent rain or a heavy shower."13 The heavy rain which covered the earth in Noah's day was geshem.

> *And the rain was upon the earth forty days and forty nights Genesis 7:12 KJV*

The heavy rain that fell in the days of Noah came as a judgment against the wicked. It was not mowreh or a yarah rain. The third rain is a repeat of mowreh. "Malqowsh, the fourth rain stands for latter rain which is the spring rain or the March and April rains which mature the crops of Palestine." 14

The fourth rain brought maturity. When crops mature a harvest draws near. Matter of fact he promised, "The former rain, (mowreh) and the latter rain (malqowsh) in the first month. This produces a supernaturally quick harvest. Not only would God release a quick harvest, but the Lord promised to restore "years that the locust hath eaten" from his people (Joel 2:23).

Joel's prophecy called for repentance like all the rest. When God's people listened, changed their minds and turned their hearts back to him, God restored his plan for their life. This includes the reestablishment of individual dreams and visions.

> *23Be glad then, ye children of Zion, and rejoice in the LORD your God: for he hath given you the former rain moderately, and he will cause to come down for you the rain, the former rain, and the latter rain in the first month. 24And the floors shall be full of wheat, and the fats shall overflow with wine and oil. 25And I will restore to you the years that the locust hath eaten, the cankerworm, and the caterpiller, and the palmerworm, my great army which I sent among you. 26And ye shall eat in plenty, and be satisfied, and praise the name of the LORD your God, that hath dealt wondrously with you: and my people shall never be ashamed. 27And ye shall know that I am in the midst of Israel, and that I am the LORD your God, and none else: and my people shall never be ashamed. 28And it shall come to pass afterward, that I will pour out my spirit upon all flesh; and your sons and your daughters shall prophesy, your old men shall dream dreams, your young men shall see visions: 29And also upon the servants and upon the handmaids in those days will I pour out my spirit. 30And I will shew wonders in the heavens and in the earth, blood, and fire, and pillars of smoke. 31The sun shall be turned into darkness, and the moon into blood, before the great and the terrible day of the LORD come. 32And it shall come to pass, that whosoever shall call on the name of the LORD shall be delivered: for in mount Zion and in Jerusalem shall be deliverance, as the LORD hath said, and in the remnant whom the LORD shall call. Joel 2:23-32 KJV*

From the New Testament Book of Acts, Apostle Peter declared the fulfillment of Joel's prophecy on the day of Pentecost.

> *1When the day of Pentecost came, they were all together in one place. 2Suddenly a sound like the blowing of a violent wind came from heaven and filled the whole house where they were sitting. 3They saw what seemed to be tongues of fire that separated and came to rest on each of them. 4All of them were filled with the Holy Spirit and began to speak in other tongues as the Spirit enabled them. 5Now there were staying in Jerusalem God-fearing Jews from every nation under heaven. 6When they heard this sound, a crowd came together in bewilderment, because each one heard their own language being spoken. 7Utterly amazed, they asked: "Aren't all these who are speaking Galileans? 8Then how is it that each of us hears them in our native language? 9Parthians, Medes*

and Elamites; residents of Mesopotamia, Judea and Cappadocia, Pontus and Asia, 10Phrygia and Pamphylia, Egypt and the parts of Libya near Cyrene; visitors from Rome 11(both Jews and converts to Judaism); Cretans and Arabs—we hear them declaring the wonders of God in our own tongues!"12Amazed and perplexed, they asked one another, "What does this mean?" 13Some, however, made fun of them and said, "They have had too much wine." Acts 2:1-13

14Then Peter stood up with the Eleven, raised his voice and addressed the crowd: "Fellow Jews and all of you who live in Jerusalem, let me explain this to you; listen carefully to what I say. 15These people are not drunk, as you suppose. It's only nine in the morning! 16No, this is what was spoken by the prophet Joel: 17" 'In the last days, God says, I will pour out my Spirit on all people. Your sons and daughters will prophesy, your young men will see visions, your old men will dream dreams. 18Even on my servants, both men and women, I will pour out my Spirit in those days, and they will prophesy. 19I will show wonders in the heavens above and signs on the earth below, blood and fire and billows of smoke. 20The sun will be turned to darkness and the moon to **blood before the coming of the great and glorious day of the Lord. 21And everyone who calls on the name of** *the Lord will be saved.' Acts 2:14-20*

1. "H4175 - mowreh - Strong's Hebrew Lexicon (KJV)." Blue Letter Bible. Web. 12 Apr, 2018. <https://www.blueletterbible.org//lang/lexicon/lexicon.cfm?Strongs=H4175&t=KJV>.

2. Ibid.

3. "H3384 - yarah - Strong's Hebrew Lexicon (KJV)." Blue Letter Bible. Web. 12 Apr, 2018. <https://www.blueletterbible.org//lang/lexicon/lexicon.cfm?Strongs=H3384&t=KJV>.

4. "H6666 - tsĕdaqah - Strong's Hebrew Lexicon (KJV)." Blue Letter Bible. Web. 28 Aug, 2016. <https://www.blueletterbible.org//lang/lexicon/lexicon.cfm?Strongs=H6666&t=KJV>.

5. "H6010 - `emeq - Strong's Hebrew Lexicon (KJV)." Blue Letter Bible. Web. 27 Aug, 2016. <https://www.blueletterbible.org//lang/lexicon/lexicon.cfm?Strongs=H6010&t=KJV>.

6. "valley". Dictionary.com Unabridged. Random House, Inc. 28 Aug. 2016. <Dictionary.comhttp://www.dictionary.com/browse/valley>.

7. "H1056 - Baka' - Strong's Hebrew Lexicon (KJV)." Blue Letter Bible. Web. 26 Aug, 2016. <https://www.blueletterbible.org//lang/lexicon/lexicon.cfm?Strongs=H1056&t=KJV>.

8. H6010 - `emeq - Strong's Hebrew Lexicon (KJV)." Blue Letter Bible. Web. 27 Aug, 2016. <https://www.blueletterbible.org//lang/lexicon/lexicon.cfm?Strongs=H6010&t=KJV>.

9. "H6062 - `Anaqiy - Strong's Hebrew Lexicon (KJV)." Blue Letter Bible. Web. 27 Aug, 2016. <https://www.blueletterbible.org//lang/lexicon/lexicon.cfm?Strongs=H6062&t=KJV>.

10. Ibid,

11. "H4175 - mowreh - Strong's Hebrew Lexicon (KJV)." Blue Letter Bible. Web. 26 Aug, 2016. <https://www.blueletterbible.org//lang/lexicon/lexicon.cfm?Strongs=H4175&t=KJV>.

12. "H4175 - mowreh - Strong's Hebrew Lexicon (KJV)." Blue Letter Bible. Web. 26 Aug, 2016. <https://www.blueletterbible.org//lang/lexicon/lexicon.cfm?Strongs=H4175&t=KJV>.

13. "H4175 - mowreh - Strong's Hebrew Lexicon (KJV)." Blue Letter Bible. Web. 26 Aug, 2016. <https://www.blueletterbible.org//lang/lexicon/lexicon.cfm?Strongs=H4175&t=KJV>.

14. "H4456 - malqowsh - Strong's Hebrew Lexicon (KJV)." Blue Letter Bible. Web. 19 Aug, 2016.. .<https://www.blueletterbible.org//lang/lexicon/lexicon.cfm?Strongs=H4456&t=KJV>

Chapter 20

Let It Rain

Hosea prophesied using the terms the latter and former rain just like Joel. God sent this promise to many generations. He repeats this promise to us today.

> *3 Then shall we know, if we follow on to know the LORD: his going forth is prepared as the morning; and he shall come unto us as the rain, as the latter and former rain unto the earth.* Hosea 6:3 KJV

"We shall know if we follow on to know the LORD" (Hosea 6:3). Follow in Hebrew, radaph means, "to follow after earnestly, to pursue."1. "Know" each time in this verse, is yada "to perceive, to acquire knowledge, to know, to be acquainted." 2 'Following to know him' must be ongoing, much like the closeness required for a healthy marriage. I may know someone by name or by sight without ever really knowing them as an individual. My depth of personal knowledge varies among people. This depends on one's relationship with another. People come and go in one's life. This should not be in a relationship with the Lord. Did the reader catch the "if" involved in this prophesy?

"If" proves to be an important word here. After the resurrection of Jesus from the grave he appeared to more than 500 people (1 Cor. 15:6). On the day of Pentecost, only 120 people were in place to receive what the Lord promised.

> *3 He (Jesus) presented himself alive to them after his suffering by many proofs, appearing to them during forty days and speaking about the Kingdom of God. 4 And while staying with them he ordered them not to depart from Jerusalem, but to wait for the promise of the Father, which, he said, "you heard from me ... Acts 1:3-4 ESV*

> *14 All these with one accord were devoting themselves to prayer, together with the women and Mary the mother of Jesus, and his brothers. 15 In those days Peter stood up among the brothers (the company of persons was in all about 120) ...Acts 1:14-15 ESV*

> *6 Then he appeared to more than five hundred brothers at one time, most of whom are still alive, though some have fallen asleep. 1 Corinthians 15:6 ESV*

One hundred and twenty people remained in Jerusalem as Jesus commanded in Acts 1:15. What happened to over 300 people? They did not show up. When the Lord awakens the reader make sure you respond to what he requests of you. As one does "follow on to know the Lord, then pay attention," He shall come unto us as the rain (Hosea 6:3). Allow that to sink in: He comes as the rain. God shows up in our lives, in our nation, to rain upon us.

So let's find out more about this sure rain from the Lord. The term latter, "malqowsh, represents the spring rains of March and April and is the same word in Joel 2:23.3 The Hebrew word for former rain yarah was previously covered in Hosea 10:12. Recall yarah's definition "to throw, shoot, cast and pour." Not only this, but it also meant "to teach."4 God will come and teach and instruct and direct your steps, whatever one needs in a walk with him. God will answer our prayers. His rain provides whatever each one of us needs to produce a harvest of righteousness.

Pay attention to the faithfulness of his coming. "His going forth is prepared as the morning," and the morning comes around every 24 hours (Hosea 6:3). Not only is he the rain, but he is the later and former rain. Not only does the latter rain come, but the former rain does too. The Lord shall absolutely come unto us as the rain if we continue to follow after him just as the latter and former rain comes upon the earth.

Such is a confirmation of what God will do for those who apply his word in their lives. Just as spring rain falls from heaven, so God will rain upon us. He will bring a harvest of righteousness into our lives. Such a crop fulfills the purpose for which God sent the rain. This means God will bring fulfillment to his divine purposes in one's life. He will bring fulfillment to his purposes in the nations on earth.

At the time of the first rain, it was God and Adam walking in unity. Recall what the first rain provided Adam: everything good. And it was a good God who caused it to happen. Adam walked in righteousness, and God did not withhold anything good from him.

My Prayer for the Reader

Heavenly Father, I lift up those who have taken the time to read *Revival Let it Rain*. May revelation from your word penetrate their understanding as you draw them closer to you. I pray for the rain of revival to fall in every aspect of the plan of God for their lives. I pray this in the Name of Jesus and thank you it shall surely come to pass.

To the Reader, Let the Revival Begin.

Revival Let It Rain

Revival Keys

Hosea 10:12

Sow to yourselves in righteousness, reap in mercy; break up your fallow ground: for [it is] time to seek the LORD, till he come and rain righteousness upon you. Hosea 10:12 KJV

Righteousness comes out a relationship with our good God. At times we may become more religious and forget we can grow in knowing the Lord. My suggestion to the reader: take the Revival Keys into ones prayer closet. Ask the Lord what he wants to reveal to you through Hosea 10:12. God is good, enjoy the journey.

Sow to yourselves in righteousness

> Revival Key #1 - Hosea told God's children to truly turn their hearts back to their righteous God and plant seeds of doing what was right (in conduct and character) according to God's standards. The process begins when each person examines themselves and their relationship with the Lord. How is it? Can it be better? Is the reader's relationship with him cold, lukewarm or hot (Rev 3:18)?

Reap in mercy

> Revival Key # 2 - Sow righteousness and the harvest of mercy will surely come one's way.

Break up your fallow ground

> Revival Key #3 - Examine one's life with the help of the Holy Spirit to reveal any person who represents a thorn. Also explore life's worries, riches, and pleasure choking one's fruitfulness." Make the necessary changes as the Holy Spirits leads.

> Revival Key #4 – Forgive - Forgiving others and even ourselves of wrongdoing will set us free. "For if you forgive other people when they sin against you, your heavenly Father will also forgive you. But if you do not forgive others their sins, your Father will not forgive your sins" (Matthew 6:14-15).

For [it is] time to seek the LORD

> Revival Key #5 – Earnestly seek God through prayer and worship.

Till he come and rain righteousness upon you
Nations with benefit

> Revival Key #6 -.When one earnestly seeks the Lord, he sends revival rain. Just as wages are paid, the Lord rewards those who earnestly seek him. "

> Revival Key #7 - God looks upon the individual who has turned to righteousness with his mercy. Then he requires a breaking up and away of what is in the way of fruitfulness. When done, now he rains upon them. This is not only what happens to an individual, but for the nation of the people. When God's people turn to righteousness, then their nation can reap the benefit of righteousness in government (judges and rulers). When he sends the rain, a harvest of righteousness, results in one's life.

Intercession

Revival Key #8 – Intercession - Stand in the gap as did Daniel. Pray for one's region (city, county, state, and nation). As the righteous people of God, stand on his word for our nation. He is faithful and just to watch his word to perform it.

Revival Key #9 - "Pray in the Spirit at all times and on every occasion. Stay alert and be persistent in your prayers for all believers everywhere" (Ephesians 6:18). "For if I pray in a tongue, my spirit prays, but my mind is unfruitful. 15So what shall I do? I will pray with my spirit, but I will also pray with my understanding;   1 Corinthians 14:14

Get in the Presence of God Daily

Revival Key #10 – Get in the Presence of God daily. Allow ones love relationship with him to flourish. Make sure to hear and follow his instructions.

Revival Let It Rain